50 Japanese Dishes for the House

By: Kelly Johnson

Table of Contents

- Chicken Teriyaki
- Tonkatsu
- Miso Soup
- Sushi Rolls
- Tempura
- Yakitori
- Okonomiyaki
- Onigiri
- Ramen
- Udon Noodle Soup
- Soba Noodles
- Tamagoyaki
- Karaage (Japanese Fried Chicken)
- Oyakodon
- Sukiyaki
- Shabu-Shabu
- Gyoza

- Chawanmushi
- Unagi Donburi
- Nikujaga
- Takoyaki
- Agedashi Tofu
- Zaru Soba
- Katsu Curry
- Japanese Potato Salad
- Bento Box
- Hiyayakko (Cold Tofu)
- Miso-glazed Eggplant
- Yaki Onigiri
- Tofu Dengaku
- Sashimi
- Hayashi Rice
- Kabocha Nimono
- Tsukemono (Pickled Vegetables)
- Japanese Curry Rice
- Buta Kakuni

- Kinpira Gobo
- Tamago Kake Gohan
- Taiyaki
- Chirashi Sushi
- Negimaki
- Oden
- Chikuzenni
- Kiritanpo
- Shioyaki (Salt-grilled Fish)
- Mentaiko Pasta
- Katsu Sando
- Yakisoba
- Goma-ae
- Dashimaki Tamago

Chicken Teriyaki

Ingredients:

- 2 boneless chicken thighs
- 1/4 cup soy sauce
- 2 tbsp mirin
- 2 tbsp sake
- 1 tbsp sugar
- 1 tbsp vegetable oil

Instructions:

1. Mix soy sauce, mirin, sake, and sugar to make teriyaki sauce.
2. Heat oil in pan, cook chicken until browned and cooked through.
3. Pour sauce over chicken and simmer until thickened.
4. Slice and serve over rice.

Tonkatsu (Japanese Pork Cutlet)

Ingredients:

- 4 pork loin cutlets
- Salt and pepper
- 1/2 cup flour
- 1 egg, beaten
- 1 cup panko breadcrumbs
- Vegetable oil for frying

Instructions:

1. Season pork with salt and pepper.
2. Coat in flour, dip in egg, then coat in panko.
3. Heat oil and fry pork until golden and cooked through, about 3-4 minutes per side.
4. Drain on paper towels and slice. Serve with tonkatsu sauce.

Miso Soup

Ingredients:

- 4 cups dashi stock
- 3 tbsp miso paste
- 1/2 cup cubed tofu
- 2 green onions, sliced
- Wakame seaweed (optional)

Instructions:

1. Heat dashi until warm (do not boil).
2. Dissolve miso paste in some broth, then stir back into pot.
3. Add tofu and wakame, heat through.
4. Garnish with green onions and serve.

Sushi Rolls (Maki)

Ingredients:

- Sushi rice
- Nori sheets
- Fillings: cucumber, avocado, crab meat, raw fish, etc.
- Soy sauce, wasabi, pickled ginger

Instructions:

1. Spread sushi rice on nori sheet.
2. Add fillings in a line at one edge.
3. Roll tightly with bamboo mat.
4. Slice and serve with soy sauce and wasabi.

Tempura

Ingredients:

- Assorted vegetables and seafood (shrimp, sweet potato, bell pepper)
- 1 cup cold water
- 1 cup flour
- 1 egg
- Vegetable oil for deep frying

Instructions:

1. Mix egg and cold water, then gently fold in flour (do not overmix).
2. Dip vegetables/seafood into batter, fry in hot oil until golden and crispy.
3. Drain and serve with tempura dipping sauce.

Yakitori (Grilled Chicken Skewers)

Ingredients:

- 1 lb chicken thighs, cut into bite-sized pieces
- Bamboo skewers
- Sauce: 1/4 cup soy sauce, 2 tbsp mirin, 2 tbsp sake, 1 tbsp sugar

Instructions:

1. Thread chicken onto skewers.
2. Mix sauce ingredients in saucepan, simmer until thickened.
3. Grill skewers, brushing with sauce until cooked and glazed.
4. Serve hot.

Okonomiyaki (Japanese Savory Pancake)

Ingredients:

- 2 cups shredded cabbage
- 1 cup flour
- 2 eggs
- 1/2 cup dashi stock or water
- Toppings: Okonomiyaki sauce, Japanese mayo, bonito flakes, green onions

Instructions:

1. Mix flour, eggs, and stock to make batter.
2. Stir in cabbage.
3. Pour batter on hot griddle or pan, cook both sides until golden.
4. Top with sauce, mayo, bonito flakes, and green onions.

Onigiri (Rice Balls)

Ingredients:

- Cooked Japanese short-grain rice
- Salt
- Fillings: pickled plum (umeboshi), salmon, tuna mayo, etc.
- Nori strips

Instructions:

1. Wet hands and sprinkle with salt.
2. Take a handful of rice, place filling in center, mold into triangle or ball.
3. Wrap with nori strip. Serve as a snack or meal.

Ramen

Ingredients:

- Ramen noodles
- Broth (tonkotsu, miso, shoyu, or shio)
- Toppings: chashu pork, soft-boiled egg, green onions, nori, bamboo shoots

Instructions:

1. Cook noodles according to package instructions.
2. Heat broth.
3. Assemble noodles in bowl, pour hot broth over.
4. Add toppings and serve immediately.

Udon Noodle Soup

Ingredients:

- Udon noodles
- Dashi broth (made with kombu and bonito flakes)
- Soy sauce and mirin
- Toppings: sliced scallions, tempura, kamaboko (fish cake)

Instructions:

1. Cook udon noodles, drain.
2. Heat dashi broth with soy sauce and mirin.
3. Place noodles in bowl, ladle broth over.
4. Add toppings.

Soba Noodles

Ingredients:

- Soba noodles (buckwheat)
- Dipping sauce (mentsuyu) or hot broth
- Toppings: sliced green onions, nori, wasabi

Instructions:

1. Cook soba noodles, rinse with cold water, drain well.
2. Serve cold with dipping sauce or in hot broth.
3. Add toppings as desired.

Tamagoyaki (Japanese Rolled Omelette)

Ingredients:

- 4 eggs
- 2 tbsp dashi or water
- 1 tbsp sugar
- 1 tsp soy sauce
- Oil for pan

Instructions:

1. Beat eggs with dashi, sugar, and soy sauce.
2. Heat pan, oil lightly.
3. Pour thin layers of egg, roll up each layer, push to one side, add more egg.
4. Repeat until all egg is cooked and rolled.
5. Slice and serve.

Karaage (Japanese Fried Chicken)

Ingredients:

- 1 lb chicken thighs, cut into bite-sized pieces
- 2 tbsp soy sauce
- 1 tbsp sake
- 1 tsp grated ginger
- 1 tsp grated garlic
- Potato starch or cornstarch for coating
- Oil for frying

Instructions:

1. Marinate chicken in soy sauce, sake, ginger, and garlic for 30 minutes.
2. Coat pieces in starch.
3. Deep fry until golden and cooked through. Drain and serve.

Oyakodon (Chicken and Egg Rice Bowl)

Ingredients:

- 2 cups cooked rice
- 1/2 lb chicken thighs, cut small
- 1/2 onion, sliced
- 3 eggs, lightly beaten
- 1/2 cup dashi
- 3 tbsp soy sauce
- 2 tbsp mirin
- 1 tbsp sugar

Instructions:

1. Simmer chicken and onion in dashi, soy sauce, mirin, and sugar until cooked.
2. Pour beaten eggs over and cook until just set.
3. Serve over steamed rice.

Sukiyaki

Ingredients:

- Thinly sliced beef
- Napa cabbage, sliced
- Shirataki noodles
- Tofu
- Green onions
- Sukiyaki sauce: soy sauce, sugar, mirin, sake

Instructions:

1. Heat sukiyaki sauce in a shallow pot.
2. Add beef, vegetables, tofu, and noodles gradually, simmer until cooked.
3. Dip cooked items in raw beaten egg (optional) and eat with rice.

Shabu-Shabu

Ingredients:

- Thinly sliced beef or pork
- Napa cabbage, mushrooms, tofu, other veggies
- Kombu dashi broth
- Dipping sauces: ponzu and sesame sauce

Instructions:

1. Heat kombu broth in pot.
2. Quickly swish thin meat and veggies in hot broth to cook.
3. Dip cooked food in sauces and enjoy.

Gyoza (Japanese Dumplings)

Ingredients:

- Gyoza wrappers
- 1/2 lb ground pork
- 1 cup cabbage, finely chopped
- 2 green onions, minced
- 1 clove garlic, minced
- 1 tsp grated ginger
- 1 tbsp soy sauce
- 1 tsp sesame oil
- Oil and water for cooking

Instructions:

1. Mix pork, cabbage, green onions, garlic, ginger, soy sauce, and sesame oil.
2. Place a spoonful of filling on each wrapper, wet edges, fold and seal.
3. Heat oil in pan, place gyoza flat side down, cook until golden.
4. Add water, cover, steam until water evaporates. Serve with dipping sauce.

Chawanmushi (Savory Egg Custard)

Ingredients:

- 2 eggs
- 1 1/2 cups dashi stock
- 1 tsp soy sauce
- 1 tsp mirin
- Small pieces of cooked chicken, shrimp, shiitake mushrooms, and kamaboko

Instructions:

1. Beat eggs gently, mix with dashi, soy sauce, and mirin.
2. Strain mixture for smoothness.
3. Place fillings in cups, pour egg mixture over.
4. Steam gently for 15-20 minutes until set.

Unagi Donburi (Grilled Eel Rice Bowl)

Ingredients:

- Grilled unagi (eel), sliced
- Cooked white rice
- Unagi sauce (soy sauce, mirin, sugar, sake boiled down)

Instructions:

1. Heat grilled eel with unagi sauce.
2. Serve over hot steamed rice, drizzle with extra sauce.

Nikujaga (Meat and Potato Stew)

Ingredients:

- 1/2 lb thinly sliced beef
- 3 potatoes, peeled and cubed
- 1 onion, sliced
- 1 carrot, sliced
- 2 cups dashi or water
- 3 tbsp soy sauce
- 2 tbsp mirin
- 1 tbsp sugar

Instructions:

1. Sauté beef in pot until browned.
2. Add potatoes, onion, carrot, and dashi.
3. Add soy sauce, mirin, and sugar.
4. Simmer until vegetables are tender and flavors meld.

Takoyaki (Octopus Balls)

Ingredients:

- 1 cup takoyaki flour or all-purpose flour
- 1 egg
- 2 cups dashi stock
- Cooked octopus pieces
- Green onions, pickled ginger, tempura scraps
- Takoyaki sauce, Japanese mayo, bonito flakes, aonori

Instructions:

1. Mix flour, egg, and dashi to make batter.
2. Heat takoyaki pan, oil wells generously.
3. Pour batter, add octopus and toppings into each hole.
4. Cook, turning balls until golden and crispy.
5. Serve with sauces and garnishes.

Agedashi Tofu (Fried Tofu in Broth)

Ingredients:

- Firm tofu, cut into cubes
- Potato starch for coating
- Oil for frying
- Dashi broth
- Grated daikon, green onions, bonito flakes for garnish

Instructions:

1. Coat tofu cubes in starch.
2. Deep fry until golden and crisp.
3. Heat dashi broth, pour into serving bowl.
4. Add tofu and garnish.

Zaru Soba (Cold Buckwheat Noodles)

Ingredients:

- Soba noodles
- Mentsuyu dipping sauce
- Wasabi and sliced green onions

Instructions:

1. Cook soba noodles, rinse in cold water, drain well.
2. Serve noodles on bamboo mat or plate.
3. Dip noodles in mentsuyu sauce with wasabi and green onions.

Katsu Curry (Pork Cutlet Curry)

Ingredients:

- Tonkatsu (breaded fried pork cutlet)
- Japanese curry roux (store-bought or homemade)
- Cooked rice
- Vegetables for curry (potato, carrot, onion)

Instructions:

1. Prepare curry with vegetables and roux.
2. Slice tonkatsu.
3. Serve tonkatsu over rice, ladle curry on top.

Japanese Potato Salad

Ingredients:

- 3 medium potatoes
- 1/2 cucumber, thinly sliced
- 1 small carrot, grated or finely chopped
- 1/4 onion, thinly sliced
- 2 boiled eggs, chopped
- 3 tbsp Japanese mayo (Kewpie)
- 1 tsp rice vinegar
- Salt and pepper to taste

Instructions:

1. Boil potatoes until tender, peel and mash roughly.
2. Blanch cucumber and carrot briefly, then drain well.
3. Soak onions in cold water to reduce sharpness, drain.
4. Mix potatoes with veggies, eggs, mayo, and vinegar.
5. Season with salt and pepper. Chill before serving.

Bento Box

A **bento** is a packed meal box with a variety of small dishes. Typical components include:

- Rice (sometimes with furikake or pickled plum)
- Protein (grilled fish, karaage, tamagoyaki)
- Pickled or cooked vegetables
- Fresh fruit

Instructions:

1. Prepare several small dishes or leftovers.
2. Arrange neatly in a compartmentalized box.
3. Chill or pack for lunch.

Hiyayakko (Cold Tofu)

Ingredients:

- Silken or firm tofu, chilled
- Toppings: grated ginger, chopped green onions, bonito flakes, soy sauce

Instructions:

1. Cut tofu into cubes or slices.
2. Top with ginger, green onions, bonito flakes.
3. Drizzle with soy sauce and serve immediately.

Miso-glazed Eggplant (Nasu Dengaku)

Ingredients:

- 2 small eggplants, halved lengthwise
- 3 tbsp miso paste
- 1 tbsp mirin
- 1 tbsp sake
- 1 tbsp sugar
- Sesame seeds for garnish

Instructions:

1. Score eggplant flesh and brush with oil.
2. Grill or broil until soft.
3. Mix miso, mirin, sake, sugar to make glaze.
4. Brush glaze on eggplant, grill briefly until caramelized.
5. Garnish with sesame seeds.

Yaki Onigiri (Grilled Rice Balls)

Ingredients:

- Cooked Japanese rice
- Soy sauce or miso paste for brushing
- Optional fillings: pickled plum, salmon

Instructions:

1. Shape rice into triangles or balls.
2. Grill over medium heat until crispy and golden.
3. Brush with soy sauce or miso during grilling for flavor.
4. Serve hot.

Tofu Dengaku

Ingredients:

- Firm tofu, cut into cubes
- Dengaku miso glaze (miso, mirin, sugar, sake)

Instructions:

1. Pan-fry or grill tofu until golden.
2. Brush with dengaku miso glaze.
3. Serve warm.

Sashimi

Ingredients:

- Fresh, sushi-grade raw fish (tuna, salmon, yellowtail, etc.)
- Wasabi
- Soy sauce
- Pickled ginger

Instructions:

1. Slice fish thinly with a sharp knife.
2. Serve chilled with wasabi, soy sauce, and pickled ginger.

Hayashi Rice

Ingredients:

- 1/2 lb thinly sliced beef
- 1 onion, sliced
- 2 tbsp butter
- 2 cups beef broth
- 1/2 cup tomato ketchup
- 1/4 cup Worcestershire sauce
- 1 tbsp soy sauce
- Cooked rice

Instructions:

1. Sauté onion and beef in butter until browned.
2. Add broth, ketchup, Worcestershire sauce, soy sauce.
3. Simmer until sauce thickens.
4. Serve over steamed rice.

Kabocha Nimono (Simmered Japanese Pumpkin)

Ingredients:

- 1 small kabocha squash, cut into chunks (seeds removed)
- 2 cups dashi stock
- 2 tbsp soy sauce
- 2 tbsp mirin
- 1 tbsp sugar

Instructions:

1. Combine dashi, soy sauce, mirin, and sugar in a pot.
2. Add kabocha pieces, skin side down.
3. Simmer gently until kabocha is tender but holds shape (about 15-20 min).
4. Serve warm or at room temperature.

Tsukemono (Japanese Pickled Vegetables)

Ingredients:

- Cucumbers, daikon radish, or other veggies, sliced
- 1 tbsp salt
- 1 tbsp sugar
- 2 tbsp rice vinegar

Instructions:

1. Lightly salt vegetables and let sit 30 min to draw out moisture.
2. Rinse and squeeze excess water.
3. Mix sugar and vinegar, toss with veggies.
4. Refrigerate at least 1 hour before serving.

Japanese Curry Rice

Ingredients:

- 1 lb meat (chicken, beef, or pork), cubed
- 2 onions, sliced
- 2 carrots, sliced
- 2 potatoes, cubed
- Japanese curry roux blocks (store-bought)
- Cooked rice

Instructions:

1. Sauté meat and onions until browned.
2. Add carrots, potatoes, water, and simmer until tender.
3. Add curry roux blocks, stir until melted and thickened.
4. Serve curry over hot steamed rice.

Buta Kakuni (Braised Pork Belly)

Ingredients:

- 1 lb pork belly, cut into large cubes
- 2 cups water
- 1/2 cup soy sauce
- 1/2 cup mirin
- 1/4 cup sake
- 2 tbsp sugar
- Ginger slices

Instructions:

1. Simmer pork belly in water to blanch, then drain.
2. In clean pot, add pork belly, soy sauce, mirin, sake, sugar, ginger, and water.
3. Simmer low and slow for 1.5–2 hours until tender.
4. Serve sliced with broth.

Kinpira Gobo (Braised Burdock Root and Carrot)

Ingredients:

- 1 burdock root (gobo), julienned
- 1 carrot, julienned
- 1 tbsp sesame oil
- 2 tbsp soy sauce
- 1 tbsp mirin
- 1 tbsp sugar
- Sesame seeds

Instructions:

1. Heat oil in pan, sauté gobo and carrot until slightly tender.
2. Add soy sauce, mirin, sugar; cook until liquid evaporates.
3. Sprinkle with sesame seeds and serve.

Tamago Kake Gohan (Raw Egg Over Rice)

Ingredients:

- 1 fresh egg
- 1 bowl hot steamed rice
- Soy sauce to taste

Instructions:

1. Crack raw egg over hot rice.
2. Add soy sauce and mix thoroughly.
3. Eat immediately.

Taiyaki (Fish-shaped Sweet Cake)

Ingredients:

- 1 cup all-purpose flour
- 1 tsp baking powder
- 1 tbsp sugar
- 1 egg
- 3/4 cup milk
- Sweet red bean paste (anko)

Instructions:

1. Mix flour, baking powder, sugar, egg, and milk into batter.
2. Heat taiyaki pan, pour batter, add filling, cover with more batter.
3. Cook both sides until golden.
4. Serve warm.

Chirashi Sushi (Scattered Sushi Bowl)

Ingredients:

- Sushi rice
- Assorted sashimi slices
- Cucumber, avocado, shredded nori, pickled ginger
- Soy sauce and wasabi

Instructions:

1. Prepare sushi rice with vinegar seasoning.
2. Serve rice in bowl topped with assorted sashimi and garnishes.
3. Eat with soy sauce and wasabi.

Negimaki (Grilled Beef and Scallion Rolls)

Ingredients:

- Thinly sliced beef
- Scallions (green onions) cut into long strips
- Soy sauce, mirin, sugar for marinade

Instructions:

1. Marinate beef slices in soy sauce, mirin, sugar.
2. Place scallion strips on beef, roll tightly.
3. Grill or pan-fry until beef is cooked and glazed.
4. Slice and serve.

Oden (Japanese Hot Pot)

Ingredients:

- Dashi broth (kombu + bonito flakes)
- Daikon, peeled and thickly sliced
- Boiled eggs
- Konnyaku (yam cake), sliced
- Chikuwa (fish cake tubes)
- Hanpen (soft fish cake)
- Tofu pouches (aburaage), stuffed with mochi or plain
- Ganmodoki (fried tofu fritters)
- Optional: beef tendon or octopus

Instructions:

1. Prepare a clear dashi broth in a large pot.
2. Add daikon first, simmer until tender.
3. Add eggs, konnyaku, chikuwa, hanpen, tofu pouches, and ganmodoki.
4. Simmer gently for at least 1 hour to allow flavors to meld.
5. Serve hot with karashi mustard.

Chikuzenni (Simmered Chicken and Vegetables)

Ingredients:

- 1/2 lb chicken thigh, cut into bite-size pieces
- 1 carrot, sliced
- 4 shiitake mushrooms, sliced
- 1 lotus root, peeled and sliced
- 1 burdock root (gobo), sliced
- 1 block konnyaku, cut into bite-size pieces
- 2 tbsp soy sauce
- 2 tbsp mirin
- 1 tbsp sake
- 1 tbsp sugar
- 2 cups dashi stock

Instructions:

1. Parboil konnyaku to remove odor, drain.
2. In a pot, combine dashi, soy sauce, mirin, sake, and sugar, and bring to simmer.
3. Add chicken and root vegetables, simmer until tender and flavors meld (30-40 min).
4. Serve warm.

Kiritanpo (Grilled Rice Skewers)

Ingredients:

- Cooked short-grain rice
- Salt
- Bamboo skewers
- Optional: chicken and vegetable soup for serving

Instructions:

1. Mash cooked rice slightly to make it sticky.
2. Form rice around bamboo skewers into cylindrical shapes.
3. Lightly salt and grill over charcoal or broiler until golden and slightly crispy.
4. Traditionally served with hot chicken soup or dipped in miso sauce.

Shioyaki (Salt-Grilled Fish)

Ingredients:

- Whole fish (such as mackerel, sanma, or aji), cleaned and gutted
- Coarse sea salt
- Lemon or lime wedges

Instructions:

1. Pat fish dry and generously salt all over, including cavity.
2. Let rest for 30 minutes, then pat off excess moisture.
3. Grill over medium heat until skin is crispy and flesh cooked through (about 5-7 minutes per side).
4. Serve with lemon or lime wedges.

Mentaiko Pasta (Spicy Cod Roe Pasta)

Ingredients:

- 200g spaghetti
- 2 sacs of mentaiko (spicy cod roe), scraped out
- 2 tbsp butter
- 2 tbsp mayonnaise
- 1 tbsp soy sauce
- 1 tbsp heavy cream (optional)
- Nori strips and chopped green onions for garnish

Instructions:

1. Cook spaghetti until al dente, drain reserving a little pasta water.
2. In a bowl, mix mentaiko, butter, mayonnaise, soy sauce, and cream (if using).
3. Toss hot pasta with the sauce, adding pasta water as needed to loosen.
4. Plate and garnish with shredded nori and green onions.

Katsu Sando (Japanese Pork Cutlet Sandwich)

Ingredients:

- 1 pork loin cutlet (tonkatsu), breaded and fried
- Soft white sandwich bread, crusts removed
- Tonkatsu sauce
- Japanese mayonnaise

Instructions:

1. Fry breaded pork cutlet until golden and cooked through.
2. Spread mayonnaise and tonkatsu sauce on bread slices.
3. Place cutlet between slices, press lightly, and cut into halves or thirds.

Yakisoba (Japanese Stir-fried Noodles)

Ingredients:

- 200g yakisoba noodles (fresh or pre-steamed)
- 100g pork or chicken, thinly sliced
- 1/2 onion, sliced
- 1/2 carrot, julienned
- 1/2 cabbage, chopped
- 2 tbsp yakisoba sauce (or mix Worcestershire sauce, soy sauce, oyster sauce)
- Pickled ginger and aonori flakes for garnish
- Oil for frying

Instructions:

1. Heat oil in a pan, stir-fry meat until cooked.
2. Add vegetables and cook until tender-crisp.
3. Add noodles and yakisoba sauce, toss everything well.
4. Serve garnished with pickled ginger and aonori.

Goma-ae (Sesame Spinach Salad)

Ingredients:

- 200g spinach
- 2 tbsp toasted sesame seeds
- 1 tbsp soy sauce
- 1 tbsp sugar
- 1 tbsp mirin

Instructions:

1. Blanch spinach, then squeeze out excess water and chop.
2. Grind sesame seeds with sugar until coarse powder forms.
3. Mix soy sauce and mirin with sesame powder.
4. Toss spinach in the sesame dressing and serve chilled.

Dashimaki Tamago (Japanese Rolled Omelette)

Ingredients:

- 4 eggs
- 1/4 cup dashi stock
- 1 tbsp soy sauce
- 1 tbsp mirin
- 1 tsp sugar
- Oil for cooking

Instructions:

1. Beat eggs with dashi, soy sauce, mirin, and sugar.
2. Heat a rectangular tamagoyaki pan (or nonstick pan) and oil lightly.
3. Pour a thin layer of egg mixture, cook until almost set.
4. Roll up the omelette from one side to the other.
5. Push rolled egg back, add more egg mixture, lift rolled part to let uncooked egg flow underneath.
6. Repeat layering and rolling until all egg is used.
7. Shape with a bamboo mat if desired, slice and serve.